CHORDS AND DISCORDS

AMS PRESS
NEW YORK

CHORDS AND DISCORDS

BY

WALTER EVERETTE HAWKINS

BOSTON
RICHARD G. BADGER
THE GORHAM PRESS
1920

Library of Congress Cataloging in Publication Data

Hawkins, Walter Everette.
Chords and discords.

Poems.
Reprint of the ed. published by R. G. Badger, Boston.
I. Title.
PS3515.A894C5 1975 811'.5'2 73-18577
ISBN 0-404-11388-5

Reprinted from an original copy in the collection of
the Memorial Library of the University of Wisconsin

From the edition of 1920, Boston
First AMS edition published in 1975
Manufactured in the United States of America

AMS PRESS INC.
NEW YORK, N. Y. 10003

DEDICATION

To the loved and lost one,
To the found and loved ones,
And
To the sons and daughters of promise
Wherever they abide,
I dedicate my dreams.

"I love you because you love the things that I love."

—Elbert Hubbard.

PREFACE

Herein I make my bow to a critical public with that fear and trembling which naturally come to one attempting to bear a mere taper in a world already adorned with luminous orbs.

The unfavorable circumstances under which these verses were written can hardly justify my putting them before the public. Some were begun in my early "teens" when I was a crude, unlettered country waif and my little world stretched out just across a few acres of corn and cotton to the little creek on the further side of the cow pasture, thence back and up the lane to the old schoolhouse and back home again. Others, while resting on my indulgent hoe or freighted bag between the cotton rows; or mid the clatter and grime of railroad travel; or walking along the dusty thorofares of the town; or in such moments which I could snatch from the grinding pursuit of bread with mountains of Toil, Poverty and Hate looming big and ominous before me to mar my vision. These haunts have been indeed too common-place to invite the delicate feet of the Muses, and if they have ever deigned to rustle their wings about me, the hard realities have so engrossed me that I failed to hear them.

Yet I have always felt something singing within

me; and out in the misty ways beyond the sickening shadows and the sordid strife of the earth-clod, sweet visions of joy and love have beckoned me and soul of mine has plumed its wings to fly away.

Nothing herein is the product of mature thought or study. These verses just wrote themselves. I have merely been the instrument thru which some peculiar unknown *something* has been speaking since childhood. How near they may reach the mark of real poetry I know not, and "it is my breeding that gives me this bold show of courtesy" in offering them to the consideration of friends.

My greatest reward lies in the hope that some Chords herein struck may be the inspiration of some into whose hands they may come, and set into motion a stream of fellow-feeling, of friendship and love flowing from them to me and from me to them, thence to all the hearts that throb and thrill with the joy that makes kings and queens of this our common clay.

If I can add to the life of another just a gleam of good cheer, a tint of golden gladness, or a bubble of pure, honest laughter, I shall feel that I am helping to plume the pinions with which we wing ourselves upward.

If there be some Discords here which seem harsh to some, know that the harshest note which language owns is mild as childhood's lightest song compared with the pangs of the soul that seeks expression here.

There may be more to tickle and please in the

parrot's prattle or cuckoo's song, but there is certainly more power and purpose in the eagle's scream and the lion's roar.

The piper does not create the music; he can but blow his flute or strike his harp, and the notes which issue forth, whether they blend in harmonious cadences or quiver in rasping discords, are the voices in the soul of the instrument created by forces not his own.

If perchance there should wait a safe rest for the feet of this my infant fledgling, then "O Crito, if so it seem good to the Gods, so let it be."

And now, indulgent reader, were I Cleanthes and thou Zeus, thus would I sing: "Lead me, O Zeus, and thou, Destiny, whithersoever ye have appointed me to go, and may I follow fearlessly; but if in an evil mind I be unwilling, still must I follow."

Sincerely,

THE AUTHOR.

Washington, D. C.,
June, 1919.

CONTENTS

Contents

CHORDS AND DISCORDS

THE BURSTING OF THE CHRYSALIS

Long, long shut in this dismal cell
    I slept, I mused, I dreamed
Of things in brighter worlds that dwell,
    No poet ever themed;
I broke the sordid prison shell,
    And out on wings I beamed.

A fair world met mine eyes and lo!
    The feathered chirping throng
Had caused the world to thrill and flow
    With music sweet and strong;
The Sun set in an afterglow,——
    My heart burst into song.

THE BIRTH

When pregnant darkness ruled the pale,
    His Spirit on the darkness shone;
Chaos in travail rent the veil,——
    The morning broke, and earth was born.

OFF TO THE FIELDS OF GREEN

I was called the wayward lad,
The strangest child my mother had;
They all were loved excepting me,
The rottenest limb on the family tree.
Stubborn, selfish, so they sneer,
Rather peculiar, odd and queer,
Couldn't be loving and wouldn't obey,
Born for his freedom and to have his way.
Temper, the like was never known,
Such as a king would hardly own,
Would fight, altho in every one
Thrice whipped he'd be when each was done.
And when the time for reckoning came,
Which one it was to bear the blame,
Perhaps a lie would stain my lip,
And then beneath the chastening whip
I'd reap my dues and off I'd skip,
Off to the fields of green.

Nine stalwart boys to brave the work,
One wayward chap to hide and shirk,
Nine champions bold with pick and spade,
One dreaming youngster in the shade.
Whate'er the blame would chance to be,
It all would surely fall on me.

The mountains of the world were piled
On this peculiar thirteenth child.
Thro all the conflict firm I stood,
And bravely as a youngster could;
For thus 'tis said in every age
It is a common heritage,
That one should bear his brother's blame,
And share alike another's shame.
A witch stepped in the family pot
At times and things grew somewhat hot,
And things began to boil and bubble,
(I never liked to trouble trouble.)
My hound and I to join the chase
Would steal away and off we'd race
With yelp and yell and quickened pace,
    Off to the fields of green.

    To chase the hare, what grander joy
Can thrill the heart of farmer boy,
When skies are blue and fields are green,
And nature wears a robe of sheen,
When flowers gay and tempting shade
Combine to make the heart feel glad,
And songs of birds and brooklets gay
Combine to chase dull care away.
Mid sports of youth the summons came
To go to school. (Am I to blame
Because I saw my honored name
Inscribed upon the walls of fame?)
I left my hoe upon the farm,

The bucket fell from off my arm
Wherewith from out the hillside spring
I'd bear the liquid offering.
I proudly walked mid classic halls
Where classic lore rang from the walls,
And sweet Pierian springs sprang up
Where young ambition fain might sup
The treasured nectar from the bowl
To quench the thirst within the soul.
But while I drank to youthful dreams,
Too soon I muddied up the streams,
For I was young and youth is rude
Untamed by years of hardihood;
And so we claim boyhood careers
The scapegoat of our after years.
Demerits forty, plus three-score
Stood 'gainst my name, it took no more
To have my name (Alas! for shame!)
Erased from off the halls of fame.
I stood before the college judge,
But young ambition didn't budge,
Except to hang my head for shame
Of banishment beside my name.
The sentence read in language bold,——
My pulse stopped still, my heart froze cold:
"You are guilty, Sir, of many a flaw,
And oft have rudely broke the law,
And since you cannot keep the rule,
We now dismiss you from the school."
And since I found it hard to stay,
And had no tears the debt to pay,

I packed my bag and sailed away,
    Back to the fields of green.

    But they who strive shall never lack,
Thro mercy's plea they took me back,
And at the shrine I pledged my truth
To be no more the wayward youth.
And they who once would oft deride
The wayward boy now said with pride,
And smiling face and grateful look,
"A clever chap when with a book."
And since vacation days have come
And school is out the paths lead home,
They who once scorned the heedless lad
And called him names which sound so bad
Now think it not a sacrifice
To bend their wills to his advice.
And with reflection o'er the scene
Of bygone days I stroll the green
With dog and book and yearning soul
To reach ambition's hoped-for goal.
And yet despite the worldly glare
Of pomp and wealth and jewels rare
In all the world wherein we rove,
I boast but one, a mother's love.
And still a child to life unknown,
I'll be a man some day, I own,
And then perhaps I shall obey
The things my friends will have to say.
But long as hope rides o'er the storm
And fires of life and love burn warm,

I need no watchman on the wall
Excepting brave ambition's call.
My heart's a pilot at the helm,
No waves can my little bark o'erwhelm.
I'll bravely breast the raging waves,
And gently sail the deep dark caves,
And rise triumphant o'er the ills,——
My haven's underneath the hills.
And when the final triumph shall call
The sons of men both great and small
To give account of what they've done,
What battles fought, what victories won;
The sheep run in to the shepherd's fold,
And the goats go shivering in the cold,
May I not blush to hear my name,
May I not hang my head in shame;
But gladly take my humble share
Where all is love and all is fair,——
If I meet none save my mother there,
  Then off to the Fields of Green.

LOVE SONG

Oft I soar above the shadows where no din of strife is heard,
And I gather golden gleams of other days;
I can hear thy name resounding in each note of passing bird,
And each note is full of blessings and of praise.

And the buds of life are blooming and all nature's fair and sweet,
And the chimes are bringing music o'er the lea;
But I'd give the world of beauties for one moment at thy feet.
And to know thy heart is open unto me.

I would gather all the blossoms from the gardens of the world
To weave into a mantle for thy feet;
I would gather all the jewels from the starry vault unfurled
To deck thy gentle brow, my own, my sweet.

A CAGED BIRD

Poor caged bird, it were a shame
To shut him in from his sweet dame;
She sings heartbroken on the bough,
I hear her saddened love song now.

She calls from out the wind-tossed tree,
It melts the stony heart in me;
She calls from morn till set of Sun:
"What harm has my lost lover done?"

He beats his wings against the bars,
And dreams of woodland slopes and stars,
His airy world shut from his ken,
He droops back on his perch again.

Sweet springing grass and fields of hay,
The leafy trees and gladsome day,
The kingdoms of the flight of wing,—
But naught for him save sorrowing.

A pain shoots thro his pulsing heart,
It breaks and breaks till it falls apart;
He hides his grief and wraps his wrong
In a bubbling burst of sorrow song.

O pent-up grief! my heart doth know,
I fain would fly but cannot go;
I wait and dream of hills and stars
Till unseen fingers break my bars.

BY THE SEA

Something in the mists of twilight
  Wafted from across the sea,
Something like a voice of heaven
  Whispers sadly unto me.

And I sit beneath the willows,
  And I list to crooning dove,
And my heart is in his crooning
  As he calls his distant love.

I can hear thy merry music
  High above the surging Sea.
And it breaks upon my dreaming
  Like a wave of rapsody.

I can hear thy accents tender,
  And the whir of bustling feet,
Feel the thrill of fingers slender,
  Child-like, innocent and sweet.

And thy ringing childish laughter
  Floats upon the rippling tide,
And my heart doth send thee greetings
  Back across the great divide.

WOOING

Tell me why you yielded, love,
  To my simple plea—
Some good grace that you wot of,
  You discerned in me?

When I touched your hand, dear child,
  Passing thru the glen,
And you glanced at me and smiled—
  Did you love me then?

When upon thyself so meek,
  A rose I sought to pin—
A sweeter rose bloomed in your cheek—
  Did you love me then?

When I filled your goblet up,
  Crystal clear and thin;
You left love within my cup—
  Did you love me then?

A SPADE IS JUST A SPADE

As I talk with learned people,
I have heard a strange remark,
Quite beyond my comprehension,
And I'm stumbling in the dark.
They advise: Don't be too modest,
Whatsoever thing is said,
Give to every thing its color,
Always call a spade a spade.

Now I am not versed in Logic,
Nor these high-flown classic things,
And am no adept in solving
Flighty aphoristic flings;
So this proverb seems to baffle
All the efforts I have made,—
Now what else is there to call it,
When a spade is just a spade?

HERE AND HEREAFTER

I can see no cause for worry
'Bout a future heaven or hell,
For the thing has long been settled
And it's plain as tongue can tell;
And it's mighty poor religion
That won't keep a man from fear;
For the next place *must* be heaven,
Since 'tis hell we are having here.

IMMORTALITY

Deep down within this failing frame,
  Dwells an immortal voice;
It keeps the heart with hope aflame,
  Makes languid life rejoice.
Be true to Life and Love we must,
  That inward voice obey,
Preserve with care this sacred dust,—
  The everlasting Yea
Speaks from beneath this crumbling clod,
  To truth be true,—obey.

A MOTHER'S LULLABY

I have heard the prince of songsters,
  Pour his soul upon the air;
And have heard sweet bells of Sabbath
  Softly calling souls to prayer;
But the song that touched me deepest,
  Till I turned aside to weep,
Was the soul song of a mother,
  As she sang her child to sleep.

See her leaning o'er her nursling,
  With her soul within her eyes;
Angel-vigil she is keeping,
  With a holy sacrifice;
And the heart melts with compassion
  As she looks in love and hums:
"Hush-a-bye, your mamma's darling,
  Sleep before the sandman comes."

There's a world of tender pathos
  As she sings her "Hush-a-bye,"
Half in pity, half in scolding,
  As she tells him, "Don't you cry."
And she tells him of the sandman,
  And the goblins that are nigh,
Just to steal the naughty darling
  If he will not hush-a-bye.

Then her lullaby will soften,
  As the strain doth upward roll,
Moves you with a sad sweet gladness,
  Breaks the midnight of the soul;
And the teardrops start unbidden,
  And you can't tell reason why,
But your iron heart is melted
  In the mother's lull-a-bye.

And the little one's face will brighten
  With a witchery of smiles
That betray the meek deception
  In its witchery of wiles;
And she tucks him in her bosom,
  And to heaven lifts her eyes,
Hiding him away in Jesus,
  Ere the fearful tempests rise.

You may sing the glad hosannas,
  You may chant the happy chimes,
With their beats and bars and measures,
  And their quaint fantastic rhymes;
But the mother's song is dearest,
  Lifts you up on wings of love,
And it wakes the harp of angels
  Round the mercy seat above.

And you view the Land ot Beulah,
  In the sweetness of the song;
And the pearly gates swing open

As the mother croons along;
And she lifts her child to Heaven,
On the prayer her soul doth hum:
"Hide me, O Thou Rock of Ages,"
Ere the fearful tempests come.

CHEWING GUM

On that night the church was crowded and the preacher rose with pride,
And he preached of the creation and of Jesus crucified;
And he warned them of repentance, and the awful judgment day,
He rebuked the creeds and doctrines, preached the straight and narrow way;
And he preached sanctification, told about the kingdom come,—
But that heartless congregation sat a-chewing chewing gum.

Then the choir sang "Old Hundred" till they made the welkin ring,
Then they turned to "Rock of Ages," simply to the cross they'd cling,
And they sang of Calvary's Martyr and the blessed Beulah Land,
Till they lifted you to glory with the saints at God's right hand;
And the angels stopped to listen, all their golden harps were dumb,—
But that soulless congregation sat a-chewing chewing gum.

Then from out the "amen corner" there arose a fervent prayer,
Floating up like fragrant incense for the sinners in despair,
And it laid the world's distresses meekly down at Jesus' feet,—
You could hear the saints a-shouting up and down the golden street;
But from out each side and corner there arose a smack and hum,
For that heartless congregation was a-chewing chewing gum.

Then he called unto the sinners to get down upon their knees,
And he raised his voice like thunder in a frenzied prayer for these;
And he painted all the horrors where the imps of darkness dwell,
Plunged them deep in lakes of brimstone, chained their wretched souls in hell,
Where the damned shall be forever, where no light of day shall come,—
But that fearless congregation sat a-chewing chewing gum.

THE RECOMPENSE

One bud to bloom, one bird to sing,
One star to shine, one harp to ring,
One smile to gleam between a tear,
Is all we need to cheer us here.

To cast a smile mid scoffs and jeers,
To kiss the cheek that's scorched by tears,
To pluck a thorn, a rose to spread
Where feet of innocence may tread;
To share my crust when friends are few,—
Is all the good I hope to do.

One trusting friend is all I pray,
One star to light the narrow way;
One angel-whisper 'twixt a moan,
One trusting hand laid in my own;
No gilded mansions do I crave,
No golden streets my hopes would pave;
I fain would dwell where hearts are strong,
Where I may dream and sing my song.

THE BREAD MY MAMMA MAKES

I have tasted all the dainties that they bake across the Sea,
I have tried the snowy manna that they make in Germany,
I have dined on Scotland pancakes till I nearly hurt my side,
And have eaten nameless nothings that were rather Frenchified,—
But with all your dainty doughnuts and your curly-cues and cakes,
There is nothing half so pleasing as the bread my mamma makes.

And she kneads it, and she rolls it and she works it up and down,
Then she puts it in the oven till it looks so good and brown;
And the crust will crisp and crackle,—it's a cone-pone bye and bye,
And you are in the corner quiet, but you are watching on the sly,
For the cone-pone's smiling at you till your little side just shakes,
There is health and joy a-coming from the bread that mamma makes.

When you see the steam arising from the greasy
oven-pan,
And you try to keep from shouting just like mamma's
little man;
But your eyes commence a-blinking and your fingers
fairly itch,
And a ticklish feeling takes you, you begin to twist
and twitch,
For your little heart is bursting and your side just
shakes and aches,
There is comfort for that feeling in the bread that
mamma makes.

When you leave the dear old fireside and out in the
world you roam,
You will think about the goodies that are packed
away at home;
You can hear the pot a-singing, and you almost taste
the beans,
Then those good old greasy dumplings and those
good old greasy greens,
And your heart becomes a rebel and a homeward
bound it takes,
Nothing fills that inward yearning like the bread
that mamma makes.

Now the biscuits may be dainty that they bake along
the Rhine,
And their rolls may look like cotton, but my moth-
er's bread for mine,

For it's just so rich and greasy that it almost falls
apart,
And it wakes a ticklish feeling in the region of the
heart;
And you just can't hold it longer, for your little
heart just breaks,
For the health and joy a-coming from the bread that
mamma makes.

WAIL ON A WICKED BACHELOR

Ho, every one who would be wise,
Come, hearken to my wail;
The hero if ye should despise,
Spare him who tells the tale.

A bachelor lived in our town,
More sour than the rest;
He won distinction and renown
As one ill-tempered pest.

A selfish life this bachelor led,
Within his lone retreat;
The hungry thrice per day he fed
When he himself did eat.

He had no comforts for his lot,
No bounties he desired;
The outcast shared his humble cot
When he *himself* retired.

He grumbled with both quick and dead,
As he alone could wish;
And on the waters cast his bread,
When he went off to fish.

A proverb heard this wicked soul,
"Go to the ant, be wise;"

Straight to his aunt he went and stole
Her gold before her eyes.

At length he sought a wife to wed,
To share his ill-got pelf;
He found a wizen witch-like maid
As wicked as himself.

They growled and grumbled night and day,
Each struggling to be free;
Too much alike in every way
For either to agree.

At last she took his coffee cup,
And doped it on the sly;
And when he drank the final drop
At once fell back to die.

And when upon his dying bed,
His head bent to his breast,
He lifted up his sinking head
And made one last request.

He asked her that his money go
To bachelors who were free;
She hurled one sharp defiant "No!
I'll spend it all on me."

Once more he lifted up his head,
Defiant eye met eye;
He sprang up from his bed and said:
"Then I refuse to die."

THE RICHES I LOVE

A crust or a crumb honest labor has earned
On a board where the torches of virtues have burned,
Where the smiles of content grace the scenes as they
move,
Is the feast where I revel, the banquet I love.

A bubble of glee from the heart of a child,
A drink of cold water from hands undefiled,
A quaff from the spring 'neath the hill by the grove,
Is the wine that I drink, and the nectar I love.

The heart of a maiden whose vestures unsoiled,
Whose hands are unstained tho in poverty toiled,
Whose honor unpurchased, whom angels approve,
Is the shrine where I worship, the kingdom I love.

THE DROWSY WORLD DREAMS ON

A flower bloomed out on a woodland hill,
A song rose up from the woodland rill;
But the floweret bloomed but to wither away,
And no man heard what the stream had to say,
For the drowsy world dreamed on.

Thro the frills of a curtain a moonbeam crept,
Till it fell on the crib where a nursling slept;
And a whisper and smile lit a wee dimpled face,
But none save the angels their beauty could trace,
For the drowsy world dreamed on.

A wee bird piped out mid the corn,
A rose bloomed out beneath the thorn;
But the scent of the rose and the birdling's lay
On the winds of the morning were wafted away
While the drowsy world dreamed on.

And the drowsy old world's growing gloomy and gray,
While the joys that are sweetest are passing away;
And the charms that inspire like the picture of dawn
Are but playthings of Time—they gleam and are gone,
While the drowsy world dreams on.

ASK ME WHY I LOVE YOU

Ask me why I love you, dear,
  And I will ask the rose
Why it loves the dews of Spring
  At the Winter's close;
Why the blossoms' nectared sweets
  Loved by questing bee,—
I will gladly answer you,
  If they answer me.

Ask me why I love you, dear,
  And I will ask the flower
Why it loves the Summer Sun,
  Or the Summer shower;
I will ask the lover's heart
  Why it loves the moon,
Or the star-besprinkled skies
  In a night in June.

Ask me why I love you, dear,
  And I will ask the vine
Why its tendrils trustingly
  Round the oak entwine;
Why you love the mignonette
  Better than the rue,—
If you will but answer me,
  I will answer you.

Ask me why I love you, dear,
  Let the lark reply,
Why his heart is full of song
  When the twilight's nigh;
Why the lover heaves a sigh
  When her heart is true;
If you will but answer me,
  I will answer you.

GOD

Islam and Buddha and Christ, all but tend
Toward the same goal,—these but means toward
an end.
In the full depths or winged flights of my mind,
That which unites me to all human kind,
Links the All-Good to the goodness in me,
Makes life sublime today, not life to be,
Lifts my soul off the harsh rack and the rod,
Gives me soul-consciousness,—this is my God.

LOVE SONG

Child of the May-time,
  Buxom as June,
Pleasing as gay chime
  Of harps in tune;
Heart of mine leadeth me
  Prone to thy feet;
Blessings that follow thee
  Truly too sweet.

Lend me thy airy wing,
  Cumberless dove,
Up and away I'd spring,
  Forth to my love;
Sheltered from dire distress,
  Shielded from stings
In the sweet blissfulness
  Thy presence brings.

Moons wane and pleasures call,
  Days come and go;
If world on world should fall,—
  Nothing I know.
Worlds may their charge fulfill
  Or faithless prove;
Faithful I follow still
  Pleasures of love.

WRONG'S REWARD

It is writ in truth eternal,
And the stars of heaven tell,
That he who dares to do the wrong
Has pitched his tent toward hell;
And his steps shall lead him downward,
And his tottering limbs shall fall,
And the wrath of the Avenger
Shall surround him like a pall.

It was sung at earth's awakening,
'Twill be sung when earth is past,
That the cup of worldly pleasure
Is embittered at the last.
'Tis more deeply still recorded,
Dread injunction 'gainst the strong,
Men like autumn leaves shall tremble
When they dare to do the wrong.

Decked with thorns the right may suffer,
Wrong may triumph with his crown;
At the stake the truth may falter,
Justice sees her throne pulled down;
And the retribution tarries,
And the debt may linger long;
But the dread recoil is coming
To the man who does the wrong.

King and queen may rise and revel
In the wealth of life they hoard,
'Neath their sway the slave may swelter
Underneath his master's load;
Potentates may reign in power,
Vile at heart but great in song;
But the gods hold vindication
'Gainst the man who does the wrong.

Lo! the avenging arm of Justice
Holds aloof the awful stroke;
But in pity still she stays it—
'Tis to man a mocking joke.
O, when patience is exhausted!
Wearied out redemption's song!
Men like autumn leaves shall tremble
When they dare to do the wrong.

TOO MUCH RELIGION

There is too much talk of doctrine,
Too much talk of church and creeds;
Far too little loving kindness
To console the heart that bleeds;
Too much Sunday church religion,
Too many stale and bookish prayers,
Too many souls are getting ragged,
Aping what their neighbor wears.

Too much stress upon the washing,
Whether in a creek or bowl,
Does it matter since devotion
Reigns supreme within the soul?
All the unction and the washing
That the church on earth applies,
Won't suffice to clean a sinner,
If his heart is choked with lies.

There is too much talk of heaven,
Too much talk of golden streets,
When you can't be sympathetic
When a needy neighbor meets;
Too much talk about the riches
You expect to get "up there,"
When one will not do his duty
As a decent being here.

There is too much Sunday goodness
When you gather at the church,
While next day you spurn a brother
Who has fallen in the lurch.
There is too much mournful preaching,
Preaching of the things to come,
How can you live straight in heaven
When there is crookedness at home?

And you needn't think the angels
Have no other work to do,
But to stitch on fancy garments
To be packed away for you;
For the people live so crooked,
Angels' robes will never fit,—
Let us have less talk of heaven
And do right a little bit.

THE FIRST LIE

I was but a country stripling,
Pompey was a lad, thirteen,
We as brothers played together,
Watched the cows out on the green.
Days of youth at times were sweetest,
Oft they soured into gall;
In our climb for youthful honors,
We would often have a fall.
It was in the heat of Summer,
Out beneath the orchard boughs,
Where we sat "jack-stones" a-playing
As we watched the grazing cows.
But Dame Fortune was against me,
And I lost the games somehow,
I preferred a charge of cheating,
And we fell into a row.
Stones at once commenced a-flying,
And the missiles flew apace;
When I stopped to find a swear-word,
His fist landed in my face.
Stars began at once to twinkle,
But I clinched him like a man,
And we fought and tugged and tussled
Only as two brothers can.
When the same blood meets in battle,

Sympathies are laid aside,
And we fought like two young demons,
Till each other bled and cried.
Father dropped his reins to listen,
Soon he stood as referee;
As he came down thro the orchard
He brought limbs from many a tree.
Vengeance shone on his forehead,
As he trod the orchard path;
In his face was writ our judgment,
On his brow paternal wrath.
But before he used his weapons
Both agreed by wink of eye,
To combine to foil judgment
Thro the medium of a lie.
Quick as thought the scheme was settled,
Neither of our eyes yet dry,
Pompey swore we both were playing,—
I at once confirmed the lie.
Ah! the old man stood dumbfounded,
Pallor o'er his features came,
Knowing we had broke his teaching
And had lied to hide the same.
But we clung to our decision,
Nothing then could disunite;
"But," said he, "you both were crying,
And there must have been a fight."
"Father, we have not been fighting,
We were playing and at peace,
And the water you discover
Must have come down off the trees."

"If you rascals can afford to
Look at me and tell such lies,
I am too amazed to whip you!"
And he left us in surprise.

APOTHEOSIS

She was a type of what mortals call charms,
With wavelets of snow on her shoulders and arms;
Her tresses dropped down in caresses and waves,
And the things we call men meekly fell down as
slaves;
But seekers of beauty she failed to allure,—
O zealous idolaters, her heart was not pure.

The delicate tint of the lily's fair plush
Was wed to the hue of the rose in her blush;
And the sheen of the stars was agleam in her eyes,
And she bore all the charms cunning art could de-
vise,—
But art lost its magic and beauty its lure,—
O zealous idolaters, her heart was not pure.

A FESTIVAL IN CHRISTENDOM

And it was in a Christian land,
With freedom's towers on every hand,
Where shafts to civic pride arise
To lift America to the skies.
And it was on a Sabbath day,
While men and women went to pray,
Well-groomed in fashion's bright design,
Right proudly wending to their shrine.
The bell up in the steeple spoke,
Its ringing notes the silence broke,
And on the pulsing Sabbath air
Poured out its chimes, a call to prayer.
He passed the crowd in humble mode
While going to his meek abode.
From out the crowd arose a cry,
And epithets began to fly;
And so this Christian mob did turn
From prayer to rob, to lynch and burn.
A victim helplessly he fell
To tortures truly kin to hell;
They bound him fast and strung him high,
Then cut him down lest he should die
Before their energy was spent
In torturing to their heart's content.
They tore his flesh and broke his bones,

And laughed in triumph at his groans;
They chopped his fingers, clipped his ears
And passed them round as souvenirs.
They bored hot irons in his side
And reveled in their zeal and pride;
They cut his quivering flesh away
And danced and sang as Christians may;
Then from his side they tore his heart
And watched its quivering fibres dart.
And then upon his mangled frame
They piled the wood, the oil and flame.
Lest there be left one of his creed,
One to perpetuate his breed;
Lest there be one to bear his name
Or build the stock from which he came,
They dragged his bride up to the pyre
And plunged her headlong in the fire,
Full-freighted with an unborn child,
Hot embers on her form they piled.
And then they raised a Sabbath song,
The echo sounded wild and strong,
A benediction to the skies
That crowned the human sacrifice.
A little boy stepped out the crowd,
His face was pale, his accents loud:
"My ma could not get to the fun,
And so I came, her youngest son,
To get the news of what went on."
He stirred the ashes, found a bone,—
(A bit of flesh was hanging on.)

He bore it off a cherished prize,
A remnant of the sacrifice.

And this where men are civilized,
Where culture is so highly prized;
Where liberty with blood was bought,
And all the "Christian virtues" taught,
Where nations boast their God has sent
The angel of Enlightenment.
But while you sing your country's pride
Where men for liberty have died,
Compare the strain with double stress
To her reward for harmlessness,
When burning flesh makes sporty time,
And innocence is greatest crime.
Alas! no doubt, the heathen reads
Of Christian lands and Christian deeds;
But blest is he who never sees
Grim sacrifices such as these,
Which culture wrings from the despised
To pay for being civilized.
Blest are those souls unhurt by sounds
Of strife where love of God abounds,
Who have not learned the curse of faith
Accompanied by the curse of death;
Blest are those who know not the shame
Which Christians do in Jesus' name.
O heathen souls on heathen strand,
What think you of a Christian land,
Where Christians on a Sabbath day

Upon their helpless brothers prey,
And oft their drowsy minds refresh
Thro sport of burning human flesh?
But none dare tell who led the band,
And this was in a Christian land.

THE DEATH OF JUSTICE

These the dread days which the seers have foretold,
These the fell years which the prophets have dreamed;
Visions they saw in those full days of old,
The fathers have sinned and the children blasphemed.
Hurt is the world, and its heart is unhealed,
Wrong sways the sceptre and Justice must yield.

We have come to the travail of troublous times,
Justice must bow before Moloch and Baal;
Blasphemous prayers for the triumph of crimes,
High sounds the cry of the children who wail.
Hurt is the world, and its heart is unhealed,
Wrong sways the sceptre and Justice must yield.

In the brute strength of the sword men rely,
They count not Justice in reckoning things;
Whom their lips worship their hearts crucify,
This the oblation the votary brings.
Hurt is the world, and its heart is unhealed,
Wrong sways the sceptre and Justice must yield.

Locked in death-struggle humanity's host,
Seeking revenge with the dagger and sword;

This is the pride which the Pharisees boast,
Man damns his brother in the name of his Lord.
Hurt is the world, and its heart is unhealed,
Wrong sways the sceptre and Justice must yield.

Time dims the glare of the pomp and applause,
Vain-glorious monarchs and proud princes fall;
Until the death of Time revokes his laws,
His awful mandate shall reign over all.
Hurt is the world, and its heart is unhealed,
Wrong sways the sceptre and Justice must yield.

LAND OF THE LIVING LIE

Now they preach and pray "good will to men,"
  And they sing of "peace on earth,"
And they tell of the joys when millennium dawns,
  And the new pentecostal birth;
But the children weep in their broken sleep,
  For hunger is gnawing within;
And the helpless hosts go by like ghosts
  To grind in the marts of men.

And the birds of prey pick the bones by the way
  Where the burdened souls sink down;
They knelt in prayer and they perished there,
  And they wore a cross for a crown.
But the revelers dance on the hills away
  Where the lights are sparkling high;
And life's too dear for the poor to pay
  In the land of the Living Lie.

And the belching guns and the cannon's boom
  Shriek loud mid the hell of war;
And the grist in the mills is the souls of men
  That are stuffed in the grinding maw.
And the sweetheart's sighs and the mother's moans,
  And the lisping children's cry
Are silenced all in the maddening din
  In the land of the Living Lie.

And the barns are full and the presses burst
  With the grapes full ripe with wine;
But the feasts are pawns of the thieves and lords,
  Not the toiler's meed nor mine.
But Mammon's mills will cease to grind
  When the grist in the mills runs by,
Then the grinders all will grind themselves
  In the land of the Living Lie.

EVOLUTION

Scientific men declare
  That man from monkey came,
But prided Christian minds regard
  The theory with shame,
And marvel that presumptuous men
  Blaspheme Jehovah's name.

And men who hold these varied views
  With arguments have tried,
And clashed on learning's battle-ground
  To justify their side;
But when at last could not agree
  Each said the other lied.

And theologs have spent their oil
  And spared no search nor pain
To cement all the scattered links
  Throughout creation's chain
To put to naught the theory
  The scientists maintain.

The horse began the size of fox,
  At first his toes were five,
Alike through years the lower forms
  To higher forms arrive;

And in the strife of weak and strong
  The fittest will survive.

The weaker creatures died out
  Beneath their stronger foe,
Who metamorphosed himself somewhat
  As upward he did grow—
Thus parent-stocks were modified,
  Zoology will show.

Fair Science still comes to our aid,
  We find as we pursue,
The *flea* into *grasshopper* jumped,
  Then *frog*—and on he grew
To *flying-squirrel*—*opossum* next—
  Then into *kangaroo.*

And musing o'er his helpless state,
  The poor disgruntled *snail*
Leaped in the water and became
  A thing of more avail;
He changed to *minnow,*—*shad*—then *shark,*—
  To *porpoise*—into *whale.*

The *lightning-bug* bemoaned his size,
  A change he underwent,
He grew to *humming-bird,*—then *quail,*
  But still was discontent;
Became a *duck,*—a *peacock* next,—
  And then to *ostrich* went.

And even so man might have been
  An insect or a worm;
No higher thought could he conceive
  Except to eat and squirm,
Till one day eating he grew fat,
  And found his voice was firm.

Then evolution soon commenced
  And, growing fast, began
From *worm* to *mouse*—then *rat*—then *fox,*—
  (From speck into a span)
And up he climbed—to *wolf*—then *dog,*—
  Then *monkey*—into *man.*

Then speaks in wrath the theolog
  The scientists to damn;
"Your reasoning is blasphemy,
  Your theory a sham;
You may be monkeys grown from worms,—
  God made me as I am."

Let wizards wrangle and dispute,
  The wise may fume and fret;
But still despite how man came forth,
  One cannot well forget,
The evolution's incomplete,—
  For man's a monkey yet!

IN SPITE OF DEATH

Curses come in every sound,
And wars spread gloom and death around.
The cannon belch forth death and doom,
But still the lilies wave and bloom.
Man fills the earth with grief and wrong,
But cannot hush the bluebird's song;
My stars are dancing on the sea,
The waves fling kisses up at me.
Each night my gladsome moon doth rise,
A rainbow gilds my evening skies;
The robin's song is full and fine,
And lilies lift their lips to mine.

The jonquils ope their petals sweet,
The poppies dance around my feet;
In spite of winter and of death,
The spring is in the zephyr's breath.

THE GOODY GOODY GOOD

Ye all, no doubt, have been deceived
  By goody goody people,
Whose good professions were as high
  As some cathedral steeple;
In whose pure eyes your faults did rise
  Like spectres grim and gory,
While these masked devils in disguise
  Wore gilded robes of glory.

If you would see these pious souls
  Just go to some church meeting;
They congregate to praise themselves,
  Like sinless lambs a-bleating;
They tell their Lord how pure they are
  With eloquence expanding,—
Most pious saints upon their knees,
  But devils when they're standing.

They tell their Lord of all the sins
  Their neighbors have committed,
Then ask for wings, gold shoes and crowns,—
  (The crooked can't be fitted.)
It seems the Lord can't understand
  The language they are using,
For never has He answered yet,
  Nor heeded their abusing.

They sing of fields where manna grows,
  And hallelujah-halley,—
Ambrosial things on heavenly trees
  In hallelujah valley;
"Saints of the Lord" they call themselves
  And sing of peace and plenty,
Tho earth ne'er had one day of peace
  Nor food for one in twenty.

Once there were people just and wise,
  Devoid of false conventions,
Nor did they look with evil eyes
  Upon their friends' intentions;
But they have died, their spirits bide
  With ghosts up in the steeple,
And I must still contend and fret
    With goody goody people.

When sheaves of plenty filled my store
  And peace my way attended,
Right readily the pious pure
  Unto my store-house wended;
And then misfortune dogged my steps,
  And friends I sorely needed,
I sought these heaven-aspiring doves
  And my misfortunes pleaded.

They came forsooth with tear-stained eyes
  And looked upon my sorrow:
"Do not despair, O brother mine,
  We will return tomorrow."

That hoped-for morrow never came,
  My heavy heart still yearning;
The path that led those saints away
  Has never known a turning.

They left their prayers, their songs, their tears,
  And that is all they left me,—
A somewhat briny feast forsooth
  With all my hopes bereft me;
Their vocal salve upon my head
  Has never made me younger,
And not a prayer they ever said
  Has ever eased my hunger.

When comes my time to pay that debt
  Which long I have been owing,
And I must board my little bark
  And set my sails for rowing;
I want no golden streets nor robes,
  Nor home with gilded steeple,—
All I desire is to be free
  From goody goody people.

THE STRUGGLE OF THE AGE

Now the cry goes forth from the heart of the world
That is hurt by the prick of the sword,
And legions of men in confusion are hurled
Where the blood of the nations is poured.

It is up and away to the call of the years,
And the heart leaps up all afire;
And the struggle goes on mid the wreck and the tears,
And the death of the world heaping higher.

On, on to the heights, for they tower the sky,
The tense throng rushes in pain;
They dash, do, and dare, no time to ask why,
"We must get, we must grab, we must gain."

It is march, march, march, to the call of the drum,
The weak are pushed out of the race;
And the soul grows sick of the hideous hum,
While the maddened rush on in the chase.

It is tramp, tramp, tramp, to the trump of the age,
The mad crowds wearily plod;
On, onward they jostle in turbulent rage,
To the temple where Mammon is God.

The sinews of life snap under the strain,
  So awful the tension they bear;
Still deepens the conflict the summit to gain,
  The spoils of the summit to share.

They get to the summit. The opposite side
  Is reeking with sorrow and sin;
They totter and fall, all shattered their pride
  As the boasts of discredited men.

Far better the abode in the peace by the road,
  Away from the strife and the sin;
And meekly toil on for humanity's good
  Than the crown of discredited men.

RELIGION

I hold no dogmas and no creeds,
It recks me not what be thy faith;
How stands thy life, how shine thy deeds,
Dost thou e'er bless the heart that bleeds?
The hungry heart in sorrow sayeth:
Thy dogmas, doctrines scarce prevail
To save a soul or form a tale.
'Tis of thyself, and not thy creeds, I have a care.

I have no care for preachers' moans,
Nor for the prelates' studied prayer;
What need has heaven for grunts and groans,
These offerings of the churches' drones,
What benediction do they bear?
What boon to bless humanity
Is treasured up for good to thee?
What contribution hast thou made
To give men life and liberty?
Not of thy creeds, but of thy deeds, I have a care.

I have no care how men proclaim
Their piety or gifts of grace;
How fares thy absent neighbor's name
Upon thy tongue for good or blame?

Thy fellow-friend before thy face
Is lost in sin and sore distressed,
While heaven which needs thee not is blest.
What dost thou give the cause to win,
To save man from himself and sin?
'Tis of thy deeds, and not thy creeds, I have a care.

THE LARK AND THE SONG

A wounded lark had fluttered on my window-sill one night,
My heart was moved with pity by its plea;
I offered it my shelter as a solace in its plight,
With gentle hand I nursed it tenderly.

I rued the cruel fingers that had sent the cruel dart
To injure such a harmless little thing;
And in its plaintive crying that flowed from its throbbing heart
It seemed to say it had a broken wing.

I gave it care and comfort till at last its wing grew strong,
I bade it bye,—it sat in pensive mood,
As if it fain would render some sweet ditty or a song
In token of its love and gratitude.

But not a note was warbled, for too soon my bird was off,
Back to the haunts of freedom,—woods and plain,
My heart was stung with pity, but withal was loath to scoff,—
Perhaps my lark and song will come again.

The bird has flown forever, but the blessing comes to
me,
As musingly I sat the drear day long;
When Phyllis 'neath my window passed, her heart
alive with glee,
My heart cried out, "Behold my lark and song."

SO SWEET OF YOU

So sweet of you to cast a smile
When all is night and clouds beguile;
The world grows kind and friends wax warm,
And sunlight lightens up the storm.
Then all is bright and skies are blue,
Fond joys abide,—and so do you;
So sweet of you.

So sweet of you when clouds stay long
To lighten up my way with song;
My day breaks fair, no more is night,
Sweet visions loom upon my sight.
My drooping wings are plumed anew,
I mount up with the song and you, —
So sweet of you.

So sweet of you to watch and wait
My coming at the open gate;
'Tis then for me the starlight gleams,
I see the moon's deep crimson beams
In eyes a-dancing like the rill,—
Some charms do more than bless,—they kill,
They strike the heart and pierce me thro;
Was heart one half so kind as you?
So sweet of you.

So sweet of you when I can trace
The stars' reflections in your face;
Fond mystic visions from the skies
Encircle still more mystic eyes.
Blow, chilling winds, for naught I care,
One heart is warm and that I share;
And he can boast a trusty friend
When sympathetic heart-chords blend.
The clouds reveal their richest hue,
The world is kind, and so are you.
So sweet of you.

So sweet of you to laugh and sing,
Such joys attend thy welcome ring.
The attar rises from the rose,
And dreams float on each breeze that blows,
And zephyr's wings, scent-laden, fling
Their sweet perfume, and harebells ring.
No crowding care, no day to rue
When thoughts of you my way pursue.
So sweet of you.

So sweet of you to scoff and tease,
To tantalize and then appease;
For joys are sweeter after pain,
The Sun shines brighter after rain.
The moldering embers glow and gleam,
The hidden coals burst forth and beam;
The drooping bud is bathed in dew,—
My head's anointed well by you;
So sweet of you.

So sweet of you to fret and pout,
To feign contempt, to fleer and flout,
With puckered lips too sweet to kiss,
Defiant eyes that veil the bliss
Which thou withholdest for awhile
To gild the sweet forth-coming smile.
That rougish glance my heart doth woo,
And play the childish peek-a-boo.
So sweet of you.

LOVE'S UNCHANGEABLENESS

The kingdoms of ages have gone,
They crumble and lie with the sod;
Like leaves their rich glories are strewn,
They return to their doom or their god.
And where is the pride of the past?
The glories of earthly domains?
They fell 'neath the withering blast,—
And yet, O yet, love still remains.

And what of fair Athens and Rome,
The pride that they once boasted of?
They fade as the beat of the drum,
Like wax in the flame they dissolve,
And Babel to dust doth return,
The builders have labored in vain;
But fires of fair friendship still burn,
And pleasures of love still remain.

We watch the bright trend of the age,
And gather its wisdom and lore,
Commune with the savage and sage,
And snatch from dame Science her store;
But wealth and all wisdom may fail
And Want follow fast in their train,
In spite of the wreck in the pale,
The sweetness of love will remain.

THE DOWNFALL OF HAMAN

He burst into bloom like the buds of the Spring,
His rich nectar sparkled with that of the king;
He fell like the blossoms by wintry winds tossed
When blighted by death in the withering frost.

He scoffed at the humble who sat in the gate,
And worshipped the pride of his mantle of state;
The poison he mingled for souls on the brink
Turned deathly and dread ere he measured the drink.

And what the rewards if the harmless had died?
And what are the fruits of the haughty one's pride?
His wrath doth rebound in a turbulent flood,
And quenches his schemes in the schemer's own blood.

And dread Retribution doth sit at the stern;
Deceit whets his sword in his passions that burn;
He sweetens his poison with flattering glare,
And leads off his victim to death and despair.

TO A SINGING BIRD

Lo! the air is rife with music,
Far and near we hear the sound,
And the stream purls o'er the pebbles,
And the Sun spreads health around;
Crickets chirp among the grasses,
And the children laugh at play;
On yon bough my singing joy-bird
Pipes a gladsome roundelay.

Something more than earthly music
Swells the chords within his throat,
Sky-born joys and heaven-sent freedom
Interwoven in each note;
All the raptures of his bird-love
Bubble in his soulful theme,
And my heart renews its springtime
In the vision and the dream.

He is singing at the portals
Of the heavenly gates ajar,
And he showers earth with gladness
And it spreads from star to star.
Now he feels the thrill of living,
And he knows the joy of praise,
And he sends to heaven his anthems
From his heart's immortal lays.

Soulful serenades of spring-time,
Soft sweet symphonies of sounds,
All the secret joy of bird-life
In his throbbing heart abounds;
And he sings care-free and fearless,
Perched beyond earth's sin and vice,
Tiptoeing his heavenly ditty
On the rim of Paradise.

TO THE HYPOCRITE

I would rather encourage
  The infidel's creeds,
Or pardon with pity
  The meanest of deeds,
Than once coincide
  With the king's haughty airs,
Or dare to be moved
  By the hypocrite's prayers.

The man who complains
  When the world is all song,
Or dares to sit mute
  When the world is all wrong;
Who barters his freedom
  Vile honors to win,
Deserves but to die
  With the vilest of men.

I've respect for the sinner
  Standing boldly aloof;
I've respect for the skeptic
  Demanding his proof;
His sins are uncovered,
  His creeds are well-known,
If I should fall victim,
  The fault is my own;

But the man who will cloak
  In a flattering disguise,
And sacrifice Justice
  For pretense and lies,
Who tampers with Truth
  For the plaudits of men,
Has sacrificed self
  On the altars of sin.

THE WARBLER AND THE WORM

High over the vale the warbler perched,
The whole surrounding main he searched;
All creatures else he would engage,
As if the world were built his stage.
He poured his heart full out in song,
He warbled thus the whole day long,
Nor thought what time or tide might bring,
His task was but to soar and sing.

A worm was plodding in the wood,
A-hoarding in his winter's food,
And thought the warbler vain and wrong
To spend the precious hours in song.
A critic bold with voice as firm
Spoke out his wrath, thus did the worm:
" 'Twere better far for all thy kind,
O bird, to leave thy song behind,
Thy lazy lay makes thee a shirk,
The noblest duty lies in work."

The warbler paused awhile to hear
What truth the worm's dull note might bear:
"I pity thee, poor toiling worm,
Doomed to the dust to slave and squirm;
Thou crawlest the earth, thy glory ends

Where royal rule of mine begins."
And once again his lay began,
The whole gamut of song he ran.

The bird's rebuke in language gruff
Chagrined the worm to make rebuff:
"I am the monarch of the soil,
And find a comfort in my toil;
I knead the soil and work for man
That he may feed and clothe his clan;
I am forerunner of the plow,
Far less a benefactor thou."
And so the worm turned to his load.
And plodded on along the road.

The warbler proudly spread his wing,
And perched on higher bough to sing,
As if to spurn the worm's dull fee
And better show his royalty;
And conscious of a nobler pride,
He thus to plodding worm replied:
"And what is life without a song
To cheer the road you plod along?
My song gives ease unto thy load,
I do not crave the things you hoard;
My kingdom is the stretch of wing,
With royal right to soar and sing;
The realms of light and love are mine,
A kinship with the things divine;
I spurn the dismal vale you plod,
I mount up to the hills of God."

And proud to be a warbler born,
He raised his note and still sang on.

And warbling warbler warbles song,
And worming worm doth worm along;
Each conscious of superior worth,
Each priding in a nobler birth.
And man is warbler, also worm,
He soars and sings, and stoops to squirm;
He worms along to get his food,
And sings to make it sweet and good.
At morn he wrings from earth his fee,
At evening turns to minstrelsy.
Where none will toil, a sickly throng,
And worse with none to cheer with song.

TO THE HUMMING BIRD

Vision of crimson plume,
Say from whence thou dost come,
  Humming thy chorus and kissing the bloom;
Flash of the lightning's blue,
Flake of the rainbow's hue,
  Where art thou journeying, where is thy home?

Flecked in thy gilt array,
Earth has no dreams so gay,
  Gladly we welcome thee, heaven-born dream;
Emblem of comeliness,
Spirit of loveliness,
  A song would not heighten thy beauty supreme.

Then when the flowerets bloom,
Eager to have thee come,
  Then will the lily lips fain be unfurled;
Blest will thy coming be,
Gardens to welcome thee,
  Thou livest in the skyland and wingest the world.

Tidings from regions fair,
Thou dost the gardens bear,
  Stealing sweet secrets from flower lips gay;
Back to thy realms of love,
Back to thy home above,
  Back to thy darlings thou wingest away.

TO THE APOLOGIST

Who would condone the wrong,
  Or else for private gain
Speaks what his heart disproves,
  Who would his conscience blunt
And accept a lie for truth,
  Or else accept inferior place
When nature made us men,——
  Mocks the God within him,
Rebukes the highest attributes
  Which distinguish man from beast,
And makes himself less than man.

TO NELLIE

The peacock's colors gayly blend,
  He proudly spreads his gorgeous train;
A fifty-dollar hat, my friend,
  Adds no improvement to thy brain.

Thy soul's sweet self I value best,
  The beauties which within thee blend;
Wert thou in homespun gingham drest,
  I'd still claim thee a valued friend.

THE KISSING SCHOOL

Just a stone's throw from the cabin
In the village on the plain
Stands a little tumbling schoolhouse,
Where I frolicked when a swain;
There were Tom and Fred and Larney
To increase my youthful sport;
I remember at the reckoning
We all fell a fraction short.
There were lassies in the schoolhouse
Who wore softened airs of grace,
And the peach and apple blossoms
Lost their sweetness in their face.
They were young and ripe with beauty
With a subtle magic air;
I was hero when it came to
Stealing roses for their hair.
There were problems then to cipher,
There were lessons, too, to tell,
There were charms of joy and pastime
Till the schoolbell broke the spell.
And I look back o'er the pages
Of the joys that childhood bore,
And I'd give a thousand longings
Could I but recount them o'er.
But old Time has run out changes,

Many things have come to pass;
Did I think that I would ever
Take possession of the class?
Now the school is better builded,
Wears a brand-new coat of brown,
Neighbor to the one I cherish
With the doors all tumbling down.
There was never prouder monarch
Perched upon his gilded stool,
Nor was sceptre half so royal
As the rod by which I rule.
But our ruling's oft deceiving,
Privilege makes men too wise;
What we think to give as blessings
May be scandal in disguise;
This is just the way it happened;
She was but a tot of six,
I with eagle eye as master
Caught her in her childish tricks.
But alas! too hard I scolded,
Till it made the teardrops start;
How the little thing did tremble,
Weeping out her little heart.

I was filled with deep compassion,
Pity which I couldn't hide,
Sent the pupils from the classroom,
Called the little one to my side.
As a father fain would pity
His own trembling, bleeding child,
Tenderly I wiped her teardrops,

Kissed her cheek, she hushed and smiled.
Out to play the tot did scamper,
As she passed out midst the crowd,
There arose a rising tumult
With an echo wild and loud.
For the little child had told it,
And each mother's little Miss
Rushed straight back into that school-room
Begging teacher for a kiss.
So I taught no more that evening,
It was near the close of day,
Sent the pupils home in fury,
Locked my desk and went away.
But the message kept a-going,
Soon 'twas on the breezes flung,
Till it had spread thro the village,
Rolling on from tongue to tongue.
And next day my school was crowded,
Every Miss from far and wide
Thronged into my doors next morning
Like the rushing of the tide.
Mothers, sisters, maids and misses
Stood before me to explain,
That they thought they had decided
To re-enter school again;
Said they liked my way of teaching,
And the good result it brings,
Said they liked my mood and methods
And the way I managed things.
Now my school is overflowing,
And I teach the whole year long,

Have decided to enlarge it,
For it cannot hold the throng.
And my days are overcrowded,
Burdened with more work than rule,
My success is now unbounded
Since I run a kissing school.

WHERE AIR OF FREEDOM IS

Where air of freedom is
  I will not yield to men,——
  To narrow caste of men
  Whose hearts are steeped in sin.
  I'd sell the barbarous king,
  And let his goods be stole,
  Before I'd sell my soul,
  Or yield to base control
    Of vile and cruel men.

Where air of freedom is
  I will not yield to men.
  I'd rather choose to die
  Than be a living lie——
  A lie in all I preach,
  A lie in all I teach,
  While Truth within my heart
  Its burning fires dart
  To burn my mask of sin,
  I'd rather victory win
  Thro martyr's death than grin
    At wrongs of cruel men.

Where air of freedom is
  I will not yield to men.

I spurn the alms of men,
The livery of kings;
I own far nobler things.
I'd rather choose to own
The pauper's garb and bone,
The eagle's eye of truth,
The lion's strength of youth,
The liberty of thought,
A free man's right unbought,
A conscience and a soul,
Beyond the king's control,
Than be the lord of slaves,
Of quaking, aching slaves,—
Of senseless, soulless knaves,
Or seek to revel in
His ill-got wealth and fame,
His world-wide name of shame,
His liberty to sin——
  I will not yield to men.

THEY SHALL NOT PASS

On came the darkness and up rose the moon,
Shooting its rays o'er the walls of Verdun;
Forcing the gates came the Hun with his lance,
Dealing out death to the fair lands of France;
Loud boomed the cannon and loud belched the guns
From the bright dawn till the setting of Suns;
Till the fair vales turned a bloody morass,——
Spirit of France declared, "They shall not pass."

Thousands were there driven onto the wall,
Thousands were there in the trenches to fall,
Thousands who dared not their death-duty shirk,
Comrades in death when the guns did their work;
Blood-soaked and mangled, and broken their lance,—
Still waves on high the Tricolor of France.
Iron-clad defenders with spirits of brass,
They pledged their life or death,—"They shall not
pass."

Horses and men in the death struggle reel,—
Earth quivers far 'neath the rending of steel.
O the wild shriek and loud roar of the guns!
Lighting the night with ten thousands of suns.
Death is the lord in the wake of the shell,
Veiling all heaven with the blanket of hell.

Horses and cannon and men in a mass,——
Death blots distinctions out,—"They shall not pass."

Every heart echoed from Sun-kissed Calais
Down the wide stretches of bright Biscay Bay;
Thundered the tocsin o'er valley and lea,
From Flanders front to the gates of the Sea:
"Unto arms, men of France, breastplate and shield,
Lives on your altars and strength in the field."
Might to might, steel to steel melted as glass,——
Death was their recompense. They did not pass.

Ye shall not pass to-day, Fiends of Might,
Killing men's souls with your venom and blight,
Demons of Hate and Lust, Molochs of Greed,
Goading the mothers and children who bleed;
Steeled with defiance, our hearts are aflame,
Life or death pledged 'gainst the Vampires of shame;
Iron in our sinews and spirits of brass,
This be our oriflamme,—"They shall not pass."

CREDO

I am an Iconoclast.
I break the limbs of idols
And smash the traditions of men.
I am an Anarchist.
I believe in war and destruction——
Not in the killing of men,
But the killing of creed and custom.
I am an Agnostic.
I accept nothing without questioning.
It is my inherent right and duty
To ask the reason why.
To accept without a reason
Is to debase one's humanity
And destroy the fundamental process
In the ascertainment of Truth.
I believe in Justice and Freedom.
To me Liberty is priestly and kingly;
Freedom is my Bride,
Liberty my Angel of Light,
Justice my God.
I oppose all laws of state or country,
All creeds of church and social orders,
All conventionalities of society and system
Which cross the path of the light of Freedom
Or obstruct the reign of Right.

HERO OF THE ROAD

Let me seek no statesman's mantle,
Let me seek no victor's wreath,
Let my sword unstained in battle
Still lie rusting in its sheath;
Let my garments be unsullied,
Let no man's blood to me cling;
Life is love and earth is heaven,
If I may but soar and sing.

This then is my sternest struggle,
Ease the load and sing my song,
Lift the lame and cheer the cheerless
As they plod the road along;
And we see ourselves transfigured
In a new and bigger plan;
Man transformed, his own Messiah,
God embodied into man.